This book belongs to:

_____

Date: _____   *Time:* _____   *Deck:* _____

My Question:

_____

_____

_____

First Card (Reversed)	Second Card (Reversed)	Third Card (Reversed)	Fourth Card (Reversed)
☐	☐	☐	☐
☐	☐	☐	☐
First Card (Upright)	Second Card (Upright)	Third Card (Upright)	Fourth Card (Upright)

Interpretation:

_____

_____

_____

_____

_____

_____

_____

_____

_____

_____

_____

My Notes:

My Reflection:

Date: *Time:*   *Deck:*

My Question:

....

....

....

First Card (Reversed)	Second Card (Reversed)	Third Card (Reversed)	Fourth Card (Reversed)
☐	☐	☐	☐
☐	☐	☐	☐
First Card (Upright)	Second Card (Upright)	Third Card (Upright)	Fourth Card (Upright)

Interpretation:

....

....

....

....

....

....

....

....

....

....

....

My Notes:

My Reflection:

Date:　　　　　　　*Time:*　　　　　　　*Deck:*

My Question:

....

....

....

(Reversed)	(Reversed)	(Reversed)	(Reversed)
First Card	Second Card	Third Card	Fourth Card
☐	☐	☐	☐
☐	☐	☐	☐
First Card	Second Card	Third Card	Fourth Card
(Upright)	(Upright)	(Upright)	(Upright)

Interpretation:

....

....

....

....

....

....

....

....

....

....

....

My Notes:

My Reflection:

Date: _____ Time: _____ Deck: _____

My Question: _____
....
....
....

First Card (Reversed)	Second Card (Reversed)	Third Card (Reversed)	Fourth Card (Reversed)
☐	☐	☐	☐
☐	☐	☐	☐
First Card (Upright)	Second Card (Upright)	Third Card (Upright)	Fourth Card (Upright)

Interpretation: ....
....
....
....
....
....
....
....
....
....
....
....

My Notes:

My Reflection:

Date: Time: Deck:

My Question:

....

....

....

First Card (Reversed)	Second Card (Reversed)	Third Card (Reversed)	Fourth Card (Reversed)
☐	☐	☐	☐
☐	☐	☐	☐
First Card (Upright)	Second Card (Upright)	Third Card (Upright)	Fourth Card (Upright)

Interpretation:

....

....

....

....

....

....

....

....

....

....

....

My Notes:

My Reflection:

Date: .... *Time:* .... *Deck:* ....

My Question: ....

....

....

....

First Card (Reversed)	Second Card (Reversed)	Third Card (Reversed)	Fourth Card (Reversed)
☐	☐	☐	☐
☐	☐	☐	☐
First Card (Upright)	Second Card (Upright)	Third Card (Upright)	Fourth Card (Upright)

Interpretation: ....

....

....

....

....

....

....

....

....

....

....

....

....

My Notes:

My Reflection:

Date: _____   Time: _____   Deck: _____

My Question: _____
....
....
....

First Card (Reversed)	Second Card (Reversed)	Third Card (Reversed)	Fourth Card (Reversed)
☐	☐	☐	☐
☐	☐	☐	☐
First Card (Upright)	Second Card (Upright)	Third Card (Upright)	Fourth Card (Upright)

Interpretation: ....
....
....
....
....
....
....
....
....
....
....
....
....

My Notes:

My Reflection:

Date: _____ *Time:* _____ *Deck:* _____

My Question: _____

....

....

....

First Card (Reversed)	Second Card (Reversed)	Third Card (Reversed)	Fourth Card (Reversed)
☐	☐	☐	☐
☐	☐	☐	☐
First Card (Upright)	Second Card (Upright)	Third Card (Upright)	Fourth Card (Upright)

Interpretation: ....

....

....

....

....

....

....

....

....

....

....

....

My Notes:

My Reflection:

Date: _____ *Time:* _____ *Deck:* _____

My Question:

....

....

....

First Card (Reversed)	Second Card (Reversed)	Third Card (Reversed)	Fourth Card (Reversed)
☐	☐	☐	☐
☐	☐	☐	☐
First Card (Upright)	Second Card (Upright)	Third Card (Upright)	Fourth Card (Upright)

Interpretation:

....

....

....

....

....

....

....

....

....

....

....

....

My Notes:

My Reflection:

Date: _____ *Time:* _____ *Deck:* _____

My Question:

....

....

....

(Reversed)	(Reversed)	(Reversed)	(Reversed)
First Card ☐	Second Card ☐	Third Card ☐	Fourth Card ☐
☐ First Card (Upright)	☐ Second Card (Upright)	☐ Third Card (Upright)	☐ Fourth Card (Upright)

Interpretation:

....

....

....

....

....

....

....

....

....

....

....

....

My Notes:

My Reflection:

Date: *Time:*   *Deck:*

My Question:

....

....

....

(Reversed) First Card	(Reversed) Second Card	(Reversed) Third Card	(Reversed) Fourth Card
☐	☐	☐	☐
☐	☐	☐	☐
First Card (Upright)	Second Card (Upright)	Third Card (Upright)	Fourth Card (Upright)

Interpretation: ....

....

....

....

....

....

....

....

....

....

....

My Notes:

My Reflection:

Date: .... Time: .... Deck: ....

My Question: ....

....

....

....

First Card (Reversed)	Second Card (Reversed)	Third Card (Reversed)	Fourth Card (Reversed)
☐	☐	☐	☐
☐	☐	☐	☐
First Card (Upright)	Second Card (Upright)	Third Card (Upright)	Fourth Card (Upright)

Interpretation: ....

....

....

....

....

....

....

....

....

....

....

....

My Notes:

My Reflection:

Date: _____ *Time:* _____ *Deck:* _____

My Question:

....

....

....

First Card (Reversed)	Second Card (Reversed)	Third Card (Reversed)	Fourth Card (Reversed)
☐	☐	☐	☐
☐	☐	☐	☐
First Card (Upright)	Second Card (Upright)	Third Card (Upright)	Fourth Card (Upright)

Interpretation:

....

....

....

....

....

....

....

....

....

....

....

My Notes:

My Reflection:

Date: .... *Time:* .... *Deck:* ....

My Question: ....

....

....

....

First Card (Reversed) ☐	Second Card (Reversed) ☐	Third Card (Reversed) ☐	Fourth Card (Reversed) ☐
☐ First Card (Upright)	☐ Second Card (Upright)	☐ Third Card (Upright)	☐ Fourth Card (Upright)

Interpretation: ....

....

....

....

....

....

....

....

....

....

....

....

My Notes:

My Reflection:

Date: .... Time: .... Deck: ....

My Question: ....
....
....
....

First Card (Reversed) ☐	Second Card (Reversed) ☐	Third Card (Reversed) ☐	Fourth Card (Reversed) ☐
☐ First Card (Upright)	☐ Second Card (Upright)	☐ Third Card (Upright)	☐ Fourth Card (Upright)

Interpretation: ....
....
....
....
....
....
....
....
....
....
....
....
....

My Notes:

My Reflection:

Date: _____ _Time:_ _____ _Deck:_ _____

My Question:

....

....

....

First Card (Reversed) ☐	Second Card (Reversed) ☐	Third Card (Reversed) ☐	Fourth Card (Reversed) ☐
☐ First Card (Upright)	☐ Second Card (Upright)	☐ Third Card (Upright)	☐ Fourth Card (Upright)

Interpretation:

....

....

....

....

....

....

....

....

....

....

....

My Notes:

My Reflection:

Date: _____ Time: _____ Deck: _____

My Question: _____
....
....
....

First Card (Reversed)	Second Card (Reversed)	Third Card (Reversed)	Fourth Card (Reversed)
☐	☐	☐	☐
☐	☐	☐	☐
First Card (Upright)	Second Card (Upright)	Third Card (Upright)	Fourth Card (Upright)

Interpretation: ....
....
....
....
....
....
....
....
....
....
....
....
....
....

My Notes:

My Reflection:

Date: *Time:*   *Deck:*

My Question:

....

....

....

First Card (Reversed)	Second Card (Reversed)	Third Card (Reversed)	Fourth Card (Reversed)
☐	☐	☐	☐
☐	☐	☐	☐
First Card (Upright)	Second Card (Upright)	Third Card (Upright)	Fourth Card (Upright)

Interpretation:

....

....

....

....

....

....

....

....

....

....

....

My Notes:

My Reflection:

Date: .... Time: .... Deck: ....

My Question: ....

....

....

....

| First Card (Reversed) □ .... □ First Card (Upright) | Second Card (Reversed) □ .... □ Second Card (Upright) | Third Card (Reversed) □ .... □ Third Card (Upright) | Fourth Card (Reversed) □ .... □ Fourth Card (Upright) |

Interpretation: ....

....

....

....

....

....

....

....

....

....

....

....

My Notes:

My Reflection:

Date: *Time:*   *Deck:*

My Question:

....

....

....

First Card (Reversed)	Second Card (Reversed)	Third Card (Reversed)	Fourth Card (Reversed)
☐	☐	☐	☐
☐	☐	☐	☐
First Card (Upright)	Second Card (Upright)	Third Card (Upright)	Fourth Card (Upright)

Interpretation:

....

....

....

....

....

....

....

....

....

....

....

My Notes:

My Reflection:

Date: _____ *Time:* _____ *Deck:* _____

My Question: _____

....

....

....

First Card (Reversed) ☐	Second Card (Reversed) ☐	Third Card (Reversed) ☐	Fourth Card (Reversed) ☐
☐ First Card (Upright)	☐ Second Card (Upright)	☐ Third Card (Upright)	☐ Fourth Card (Upright)

Interpretation: ....

....

....

....

....

....

....

....

....

....

....

....

My Notes:

My Reflection:

Date: _____   Time: _____   Deck: _____

My Question:

....

....

....

First Card (Reversed) □	Second Card (Reversed) □	Third Card (Reversed) □	Fourth Card (Reversed) □
□ First Card (Upright)	□ Second Card (Upright)	□ Third Card (Upright)	□ Fourth Card (Upright)

Interpretation:

....

....

....

....

....

....

....

....

....

....

....

....

My Notes:

My Reflection:

Date: .... *Time:* .... *Deck:* ....

My Question: ....

....

....

....

(Reversed) First Card	(Reversed) Second Card	(Reversed) Third Card	(Reversed) Fourth Card
☐	☐	☐	☐
☐	☐	☐	☐
First Card (Upright)	Second Card (Upright)	Third Card (Upright)	Fourth Card (Upright)

Interpretation: ....

....

....

....

....

....

....

....

....

....

....

....

My Notes:

My Reflection:

Date: .... *Time:* .... *Deck:* ....

My Question: ....

....

....

....

First Card (Reversed)	Second Card (Reversed)	Third Card (Reversed)	Fourth Card (Reversed)
☐	☐	☐	☐
☐	☐	☐	☐
First Card (Upright)	**Second Card** (Upright)	**Third Card** (Upright)	**Fourth Card** (Upright)

Interpretation: ....

....

....

....

....

....

....

....

....

....

....

....

My Notes:

My Reflection:

Date: .... Time: .... Deck: ....

My Question:

....

....

....

First Card (Reversed)	Second Card (Reversed)	Third Card (Reversed)	Fourth Card (Reversed)
☐	☐	☐	☐
☐	☐	☐	☐
First Card (Upright)	Second Card (Upright)	Third Card (Upright)	Fourth Card (Upright)

Interpretation:

....

....

....

....

....

....

....

....

....

....

....

My Notes:

My Reflection:

Date: _____   Time: _____   Deck: _____

Interpretation:

My Question: _____
....
....
....

First Card (Reversed) ☐	Second Card (Reversed) ☐	Third Card (Reversed) ☐	Fourth Card (Reversed) ☐
☐ First Card (Upright)	☐ Second Card (Upright)	☐ Third Card (Upright)	☐ Fourth Card (Upright)

Interpretation:
....
....
....
....
....
....
....
....
....
....
....
....

My Notes:

My Reflection:

Date: _____ *Time:* _____ *Deck:* _____

My Question: ....

....

....

....

First Card (Reversed) ☐	Second Card (Reversed) ☐	Third Card (Reversed) ☐	Fourth Card (Reversed) ☐
☐ First Card (Upright)	☐ Second Card (Upright)	☐ Third Card (Upright)	☐ Fourth Card (Upright)

Interpretation: ....

....

....

....

....

....

....

....

....

....

....

....

My Notes:

My Reflection:

Date: _____ Time: _____ Deck: _____

My Question:

....

....

....

First Card (Reversed) ☐	Second Card (Reversed) ☐	Third Card (Reversed) ☐	Fourth Card (Reversed) ☐
☐ First Card (Upright)	☐ Second Card (Upright)	☐ Third Card (Upright)	☐ Fourth Card (Upright)

Interpretation:

....

....

....

....

....

....

....

....

....

....

....

My Notes:

My Reflection:

Date: *Time:*   *Deck:*

My Question:

....

....

....

First Card (Reversed) ☐	Second Card (Reversed) ☐	Third Card (Reversed) ☐	Fourth Card (Reversed) ☐
☐ First Card (Upright)	☐ Second Card (Upright)	☐ Third Card (Upright)	☐ Fourth Card (Upright)

Interpretation:

....

....

....

....

....

....

....

....

....

....

....

My Notes:

My Reflection:

Date: _____   Time: _____   Deck: _____

My Question:

....

....

....

First Card (Reversed) ☐	Second Card (Reversed) ☐	Third Card (Reversed) ☐	Fourth Card (Reversed) ☐
☐ First Card (Upright)	☐ Second Card (Upright)	☐ Third Card (Upright)	☐ Fourth Card (Upright)

Interpretation:

....

....

....

....

....

....

....

....

....

....

....

....

My Notes:

My Reflection:

Date: _____ Time: _____ Deck: _____

My Question:

....

....

....

First Card (Reversed) ☐	Second Card (Reversed) ☐	Third Card (Reversed) ☐	Fourth Card (Reversed) ☐
☐ First Card (Upright)	☐ Second Card (Upright)	☐ Third Card (Upright)	☐ Fourth Card (Upright)

Interpretation:

....

....

....

....

....

....

....

....

....

....

....

....

My Notes:

My Reflection:

Date: *Time:*   *Deck:*

My Question:

....

....

....

First Card (Reversed) ☐	Second Card (Reversed) ☐	Third Card (Reversed) ☐	Fourth Card (Reversed) ☐
☐ First Card (Upright)	☐ Second Card (Upright)	☐ Third Card (Upright)	☐ Fourth Card (Upright)

Interpretation:

....

....

....

....

....

....

....

....

....

....

....

....

My Notes:

My Reflection:

Date: .... *Time:* .... *Deck:* ....

My Question:

....

....

....

First Card (Reversed) ☐	Second Card (Reversed) ☐	Third Card (Reversed) ☐	Fourth Card (Reversed) ☐
☐ First Card (Upright)	☐ Second Card (Upright)	☐ Third Card (Upright)	☐ Fourth Card (Upright)

Interpretation: ....

....

....

....

....

....

....

....

....

....

....

....

My Notes:

My Reflection:

Date: .... Time: .... Deck: ....

My Question:
....
....
....

First Card (Reversed)	Second Card (Reversed)	Third Card (Reversed)	Fourth Card (Reversed)
☐	☐	☐	☐
☐	☐	☐	☐
First Card (Upright)	Second Card (Upright)	Third Card (Upright)	Fourth Card (Upright)

Interpretation:
....
....
....
....
....
....
....
....
....
....
....
....

My Notes:

My Reflection:

Date: _____   Time: _____   Deck: _____

My Question: _____

....

....

....

(Reversed)	(Reversed)	(Reversed)	(Reversed)
First Card	Second Card	Third Card	Fourth Card
☐	☐	☐	☐
....	....	....	....
....	....	....	....
☐	☐	☐	☐
First Card	Second Card	Third Card	Fourth Card
(Upright)	(Upright)	(Upright)	(Upright)

Interpretation: ....

....

....

....

....

....

....

....

....

....

....

....

My Notes:

My Reflection:

Date: .... _Time:_ .... _Deck:_ ....

My Question: ....
....
....
....

First Card (Reversed) ☐	Second Card (Reversed) ☐	Third Card (Reversed) ☐	Fourth Card (Reversed) ☐
☐ First Card (Upright)	☐ Second Card (Upright)	☐ Third Card (Upright)	☐ Fourth Card (Upright)

Interpretation: ....
....
....
....
....
....
....
....
....
....
....
....
....

My Notes:

My Reflection:

Date: .... Time: .... Deck: ....

My Question: ....
....
....
....

First Card (Reversed)	Second Card (Reversed)	Third Card (Reversed)	Fourth Card (Reversed)
☐	☐	☐	☐
☐	☐	☐	☐
First Card (Upright)	Second Card (Upright)	Third Card (Upright)	Fourth Card (Upright)

Interpretation: ....
....
....
....
....
....
....
....
....
....
....
....
....
....
....
....

My Notes:

My Reflection:

Date: Time: Deck:

My Question:

....

....

....

First Card (Reversed)	Second Card (Reversed)	Third Card (Reversed)	Fourth Card (Reversed)
☐	☐	☐	☐
☐	☐	☐	☐
First Card (Upright)	Second Card (Upright)	Third Card (Upright)	Fourth Card (Upright)

Interpretation:

....

....

....

....

....

....

....

....

....

....

....

My Notes:

My Reflection:

Date: _____ *Time:* _____ *Deck:* _____

My Question:

....

....

....

First Card (Reversed) ☐	Second Card (Reversed) ☐	Third Card (Reversed) ☐	Fourth Card (Reversed) ☐
☐ First Card (Upright)	☐ Second Card (Upright)	☐ Third Card (Upright)	☐ Fourth Card (Upright)

Interpretation:

....

....

....

....

....

....

....

....

....

....

....

My Notes:

My Reflection:

Date: .... Time: .... Deck: ....

My Question: ....
....
....
....

First Card (Reversed) ☐	Second Card (Reversed) ☐	Third Card (Reversed) ☐	Fourth Card (Reversed) ☐
☐ First Card (Upright)	☐ Second Card (Upright)	☐ Third Card (Upright)	☐ Fourth Card (Upright)

Interpretation: ....
....
....
....
....
....
....
....
....
....
....
....
....

My Notes:

My Reflection:

Date: _____ *Time:* _____ *Deck:* _____

My Question: _____

....

....

....

First Card (Reversed) ☐	Second Card (Reversed) ☐	Third Card (Reversed) ☐	Fourth Card (Reversed) ☐
☐ First Card (Upright)	☐ Second Card (Upright)	☐ Third Card (Upright)	☐ Fourth Card (Upright)

Interpretation: ....

....

....

....

....

....

....

....

....

....

....

....

My Notes:

My Reflection:

Date: *Time:*   *Deck:*

My Question:

....

....

....

First Card (Reversed) ☐	Second Card (Reversed) ☐	Third Card (Reversed) ☐	Fourth Card (Reversed) ☐
☐ First Card (Upright)	☐ Second Card (Upright)	☐ Third Card (Upright)	☐ Fourth Card (Upright)

Interpretation:

....

....

....

....

....

....

....

....

....

....

....

....

My Notes:

My Reflection:

Date: .... Time: .... Deck: ....

My Question:

....

....

....

First Card (Reversed) ☐	Second Card (Reversed) ☐	Third Card (Reversed) ☐	Fourth Card (Reversed) ☐
☐ First Card (Upright)	☐ Second Card (Upright)	☐ Third Card (Upright)	☐ Fourth Card (Upright)

Interpretation:

....

....

....

....

....

....

....

....

....

....

....

....

....

My Notes:

My Reflection:

Date: .... *Time:* .... *Deck:* ....

My Question: ....

....

....

....

First Card (Reversed) ☐	Second Card (Reversed) ☐	Third Card (Reversed) ☐	Fourth Card (Reversed) ☐
☐ First Card (Upright)	☐ Second Card (Upright)	☐ Third Card (Upright)	☐ Fourth Card (Upright)

Interpretation: ....

....

....

....

....

....

....

....

....

....

....

....

....

My Notes:

My Reflection:

Date: _____ *Time:* _____ *Deck:* _____

My Question:

....

....

....

First Card (Reversed)	Second Card (Reversed)	Third Card (Reversed)	Fourth Card (Reversed)
☐	☐	☐	☐
☐	☐	☐	☐
First Card (Upright)	Second Card (Upright)	Third Card (Upright)	Fourth Card (Upright)

Interpretation:

....

....

....

....

....

....

....

....

....

....

....

....

....

My Notes:

My Reflection:

Date: .... *Time:* .... *Deck:* ....

My Question: ....

....

....

....

First Card (Reversed)	Second Card (Reversed)	Third Card (Reversed)	Fourth Card (Reversed)
☐	☐	☐	☐
☐	☐	☐	☐
First Card (Upright)	Second Card (Upright)	Third Card (Upright)	Fourth Card (Upright)

Interpretation: ....

....

....

....

....

....

....

....

....

....

....

....

....

My Notes:

My Reflection:

Date: .... Time: .... Deck: ....

My Question: ....
....
....
....

First Card (Reversed)	Second Card (Reversed)	Third Card (Reversed)	Fourth Card (Reversed)
☐	☐	☐	☐
☐	☐	☐	☐
First Card (Upright)	Second Card (Upright)	Third Card (Upright)	Fourth Card (Upright)

Interpretation: ....
....
....
....
....
....
....
....
....
....
....
....

My Notes:

My Reflection:

Date: _____ *Time:* _____ *Deck:* _____

My Question:

....

....

....

First Card (Reversed) ☐	Second Card (Reversed) ☐	Third Card (Reversed) ☐	Fourth Card (Reversed) ☐
☐ First Card (Upright)	☐ Second Card (Upright)	☐ Third Card (Upright)	☐ Fourth Card (Upright)

Interpretation:

....

....

....

....

....

....

....

....

....

....

....

....

....

My Notes:

My Reflection:

Date: Time: Deck:

My Question:

....

....

....

First Card (Reversed) ☐	Second Card (Reversed) ☐	Third Card (Reversed) ☐	Fourth Card (Reversed) ☐
☐ First Card (Upright)	☐ Second Card (Upright)	☐ Third Card (Upright)	☐ Fourth Card (Upright)

Interpretation:

....

....

....

....

....

....

....

....

....

....

....

....

My Notes:

My Reflection:

Date: _____ *Time:* _____ *Deck:* _____

My Question:

....

....

....

(Reversed) First Card	(Reversed) Second Card	(Reversed) Third Card	(Reversed) Fourth Card
☐	☐	☐	☐
☐	☐	☐	☐
First Card (Upright)	Second Card (Upright)	Third Card (Upright)	Fourth Card (Upright)

Interpretation:

....

....

....

....

....

....

....

....

....

....

....

....

....

My Notes:

My Reflection:

Date: Time: Deck:

My Question:

....

....

....

First Card (Reversed)	Second Card (Reversed)	Third Card (Reversed)	Fourth Card (Reversed)
☐	☐	☐	☐
☐	☐	☐	☐
First Card (Upright)	Second Card (Upright)	Third Card (Upright)	Fourth Card (Upright)

Interpretation: ....

....

....

....

....

....

....

....

....

....

....

....

My Notes:

My Reflection:

Date: Time: Deck:

My Question:

....

....

....

First Card (Reversed) ☐	Second Card (Reversed) ☐	Third Card (Reversed) ☐	Fourth Card (Reversed) ☐
☐ First Card (Upright)	☐ Second Card (Upright)	☐ Third Card (Upright)	☐ Fourth Card (Upright)

Interpretation:

....

....

....

....

....

....

....

....

....

....

....

My Notes:

My Reflection:

Date: *Time:*   *Deck:*

My Question:

....

....

....

First Card (Reversed) ☐	Second Card (Reversed) ☐	Third Card (Reversed) ☐	Fourth Card (Reversed) ☐
☐ First Card (Upright)	☐ Second Card (Upright)	☐ Third Card (Upright)	☐ Fourth Card (Upright)

Interpretation: ....

....

....

....

....

....

....

....

....

....

....

....

My Notes:

My Reflection:

Date: .... *Time:* .... *Deck:* ....

My Question:

....

....

....

First Card (Reversed)	Second Card (Reversed)	Third Card (Reversed)	Fourth Card (Reversed)
☐	☐	☐	☐
☐	☐	☐	☐
First Card (Upright)	Second Card (Upright)	Third Card (Upright)	Fourth Card (Upright)

Interpretation:

....

....

....

....

....

....

....

....

....

....

....

....

My Notes:

My Reflection:

Date: Time: Deck:

My Question:

....

....

....

First Card (Reversed)	Second Card (Reversed)	Third Card (Reversed)	Fourth Card (Reversed)
☐	☐	☐	☐
☐	☐	☐	☐
First Card (Upright)	Second Card (Upright)	Third Card (Upright)	Fourth Card (Upright)

Interpretation:

....

....

....

....

....

....

....

....

....

....

My Notes:

My Reflection:

My Question:

....

....

....

First Card (Reversed)	Second Card (Reversed)	Third Card (Reversed)	Fourth Card (Reversed)
☐	☐	☐	☐
☐	☐	☐	☐
First Card (Upright)	Second Card (Upright)	Third Card (Upright)	Fourth Card (Upright)

Interpretation:

....

....

....

....

....

....

....

....

....

....

....

My Notes:

My Reflection:

Date: .... *Time:* .... *Deck:* ....

My Question:

....

....

....

First Card (Reversed)	Second Card (Reversed)	Third Card (Reversed)	Fourth Card (Reversed)
☐	☐	☐	☐
☐	☐	☐	☐
First Card (Upright)	**Second Card** (Upright)	**Third Card** (Upright)	**Fourth Card** (Upright)

Interpretation:

....

....

....

....

....

....

....

....

....

....

....

....

....

My Notes:

My Reflection:

Date: .... *Time:* .... *Deck:* ....

My Question: ....

....

....

....

First Card (Reversed)	Second Card (Reversed)	Third Card (Reversed)	Fourth Card (Reversed)
☐	☐	☐	☐
☐	☐	☐	☐
First Card (Upright)	**Second Card** (Upright)	**Third Card** (Upright)	**Fourth Card** (Upright)

Interpretation: ....

....

....

....

....

....

....

....

....

....

....

....

....

My Notes:

My Reflection:

Date: .... *Time:* .... *Deck:* ....

My Question: ....

....

....

....

First Card (Reversed) ☐	Second Card (Reversed) ☐	Third Card (Reversed) ☐	Fourth Card (Reversed) ☐
☐ First Card (Upright)	☐ Second Card (Upright)	☐ Third Card (Upright)	☐ Fourth Card (Upright)

Interpretation: ....

....

....

....

....

....

....

....

....

....

....

My Notes:

My Reflection:

Date: .... *Time:* .... *Deck:* ....

My Question:

....

....

....

(Reversed)	(Reversed)	(Reversed)	(Reversed)
First Card	Second Card	Third Card	Fourth Card
☐	☐	☐	☐
☐	☐	☐	☐
First Card	**Second Card**	**Third Card**	**Fourth Card**
(Upright)	(Upright)	(Upright)	(Upright)

Interpretation: ....

....

....

....

....

....

....

....

....

....

....

....

....

....

My Notes:

My Reflection:

Date: _____ Time: _____ Deck: _____

My Question: ....

....

....

....

| First Card (Reversed) ☐ .... ☐ First Card (Upright) | Second Card (Reversed) ☐ .... ☐ Second Card (Upright) | Third Card (Reversed) ☐ .... ☐ Third Card (Upright) | Fourth Card (Reversed) ☐ .... ☐ Fourth Card (Upright) |

Interpretation: ....

....

....

....

....

....

....

....

....

....

....

My Notes:

My Reflection:

Date: _____   Time: _____   Deck: _____

My Question: _____

....

....

....

First Card (Reversed)	Second Card (Reversed)	Third Card (Reversed)	Fourth Card (Reversed)
☐	☐	☐	☐
☐	☐	☐	☐
First Card (Upright)	Second Card (Upright)	Third Card (Upright)	Fourth Card (Upright)

Interpretation: _____

....

....

....

....

....

....

....

....

....

....

....

My Notes:

....
....
....
....
....
....
....
....
....
....
....

My Reflection:

....
....
....
....
....
....
....
....
....
....
....
....
....

Date: .... *Time:* .... *Deck:* ....

My Question: ....

....

....

....

First Card (Reversed) ☐	Second Card (Reversed) ☐	Third Card (Reversed) ☐	Fourth Card (Reversed) ☐
☐ First Card (Upright)	☐ Second Card (Upright)	☐ Third Card (Upright)	☐ Fourth Card (Upright)

Interpretation: ....

....

....

....

....

....

....

....

....

....

....

My Notes:

My Reflection:

Date: _____ Time: _____ Deck: _____

My Question:

....

....

....

First Card (Reversed)	Second Card (Reversed)	Third Card (Reversed)	Fourth Card (Reversed)
☐	☐	☐	☐
☐	☐	☐	☐
First Card (Upright)	Second Card (Upright)	Third Card (Upright)	Fourth Card (Upright)

Interpretation:

....

....

....

....

....

....

....

....

....

....

....

My Notes:

My Reflection:

Date: *Time:*   *Deck:*

My Question:

....

....

....

First Card (Reversed) ☐	Second Card (Reversed) ☐	Third Card (Reversed) ☐	Fourth Card (Reversed) ☐
☐ First Card (Upright)	☐ Second Card (Upright)	☐ Third Card (Upright)	☐ Fourth Card (Upright)

Interpretation:

....

....

....

....

....

....

....

....

....

....

....

....

....

My Notes:

My Reflection:

Date: _____ *Time:* _____ *Deck:* _____

My Question:

....

....

....

First Card (Reversed) ☐	Second Card (Reversed) ☐	Third Card (Reversed) ☐	Fourth Card (Reversed) ☐
☐ First Card (Upright)	☐ Second Card (Upright)	☐ Third Card (Upright)	☐ Fourth Card (Upright)

Interpretation:

....

....

....

....

....

....

....

....

....

....

....

....

....

My Notes:

My Reflection:

Date: .... Time: .... Deck: ....

My Question: ....

....

....

....

First Card (Reversed) ☐	Second Card (Reversed) ☐	Third Card (Reversed) ☐	Fourth Card (Reversed) ☐
☐ First Card (Upright)	☐ Second Card (Upright)	☐ Third Card (Upright)	☐ Fourth Card (Upright)

Interpretation: ....

....

....

....

....

....

....

....

....

....

....

....

My Notes:

My Reflection:

Date: *Time:*   *Deck:*

My Question:

....

....

....

First Card (Reversed) ☐	Second Card (Reversed) ☐	Third Card (Reversed) ☐	Fourth Card (Reversed) ☐
☐ First Card (Upright)	☐ Second Card (Upright)	☐ Third Card (Upright)	☐ Fourth Card (Upright)

Interpretation:

....

....

....

....

....

....

....

....

....

....

....

....

My Notes:

_____
_____
_____
_____
_____
_____
_____
_____
_____
_____

My Reflection:

_____
_____
_____
_____
_____
_____
_____
_____
_____
_____

Date: .... *Time:* .... *Deck:* ....

My Question: ....

....

....

....

First Card (Reversed)	Second Card (Reversed)	Third Card (Reversed)	Fourth Card (Reversed)
☐	☐	☐	☐
☐	☐	☐	☐
First Card (Upright)	**Second Card** (Upright)	**Third Card** (Upright)	**Fourth Card** (Upright)

Interpretation: ....

....

....

....

....

....

....

....

....

....

....

....

My Notes:

My Reflection:

Date: .... Time: .... Deck: ....

My Question:
....

....

....

....

First Card (Reversed)	Second Card (Reversed)	Third Card (Reversed)	Fourth Card (Reversed)
☐	☐	☐	☐
☐	☐	☐	☐
First Card (Upright)	Second Card (Upright)	Third Card (Upright)	Fourth Card (Upright)

Interpretation:
....

....

....

....

....

....

....

....

....

....

....

....

My Notes:

My Reflection:

Date: _____ *Time:* _____ *Deck:* _____

My Question:

....

....

....

First Card (Reversed) ☐	Second Card (Reversed) ☐	Third Card (Reversed) ☐	Fourth Card (Reversed) ☐
☐ First Card (Upright)	☐ Second Card (Upright)	☐ Third Card (Upright)	☐ Fourth Card (Upright)

Interpretation:

....

....

....

....

....

....

....

....

....

....

....

My Notes:

My Reflection:

Date: Time: Deck:

My Question:

....

....

....

First Card (Reversed)	Second Card (Reversed)	Third Card (Reversed)	Fourth Card (Reversed)
☐	☐	☐	☐
☐	☐	☐	☐
First Card (Upright)	Second Card (Upright)	Third Card (Upright)	Fourth Card (Upright)

Interpretation:

....

....

....

....

....

....

....

....

....

....

....

....

....

My Notes:

Date: Time: Deck:

My Question:

....

....

....

First Card (Reversed)	Second Card (Reversed)	Third Card (Reversed)	Fourth Card (Reversed)
☐	☐	☐	☐
☐	☐	☐	☐
First Card (Upright)	Second Card (Upright)	Third Card (Upright)	Fourth Card (Upright)

Interpretation:

....

....

....

....

....

....

....

....

....

....

....

My Notes:

My Reflection:

Date: _____   Time: _____   Deck: _____

My Question: _____
....
....
....

First Card (Reversed)	Second Card (Reversed)	Third Card (Reversed)	Fourth Card (Reversed)
☐	☐	☐	☐
☐	☐	☐	☐
First Card (Upright)	Second Card (Upright)	Third Card (Upright)	Fourth Card (Upright)

Interpretation: _____
....
....
....
....
....
....
....
....
....
....
....
....
....

My Notes:

My Reflection:

Date: .... *Time:* .... *Deck:* ....

My Question: ....

....

....

....

First Card (Reversed) ☐	Second Card (Reversed) ☐	Third Card (Reversed) ☐	Fourth Card (Reversed) ☐
☐ First Card (Upright)	☐ Second Card (Upright)	☐ Third Card (Upright)	☐ Fourth Card (Upright)

Interpretation: ....

....

....

....

....

....

....

....

....

....

....

....

My Notes:

My Reflection:

Date: .... Time: .... Deck: ....

My Question: ....
....
....
....

First Card (Reversed)	Second Card (Reversed)	Third Card (Reversed)	Fourth Card (Reversed)
☐	☐	☐	☐
First Card (Upright)	Second Card (Upright)	Third Card (Upright)	Fourth Card (Upright)

Interpretation: ....
....
....
....
....
....
....
....
....
....
....
....

My Notes:

My Reflection:

Date: .... *Time:* .... *Deck:* ....

My Question: ....

....

....

First Card (Reversed)	Second Card (Reversed)	Third Card (Reversed)	Fourth Card (Reversed)
☐	☐	☐	☐
☐	☐	☐	☐
First Card (Upright)	Second Card (Upright)	Third Card (Upright)	Fourth Card (Upright)

Interpretation: ....

....

....

....

....

....

....

....

....

....

....

....

My Notes:

My Reflection:

Date: .... *Time:* .... *Deck:* ....

My Question: ....

....

....

....

First Card (Reversed) ☐	Second Card (Reversed) ☐	Third Card (Reversed) ☐	Fourth Card (Reversed) ☐
☐ First Card (Upright)	☐ Second Card (Upright)	☐ Third Card (Upright)	☐ Fourth Card (Upright)

Interpretation: ....

....

....

....

....

....

....

....

....

....

....

My Notes:

My Reflection:

Date: .... Time: .... Deck: ....

My Question:

....

....

....

....

First Card (Reversed) ☐	Second Card (Reversed) ☐	Third Card (Reversed) ☐	Fourth Card (Reversed) ☐
☐ First Card (Upright)	☐ Second Card (Upright)	☐ Third Card (Upright)	☐ Fourth Card (Upright)

Interpretation:

....

....

....

....

....

....

....

....

....

....

....

....

....

My Notes:

Date: *Time:*   *Deck:*

My Question:

....

....

....

First Card (Reversed)	Second Card (Reversed)	Third Card (Reversed)	Fourth Card (Reversed)
☐	☐	☐	☐
☐	☐	☐	☐
First Card (Upright)	Second Card (Upright)	Third Card (Upright)	Fourth Card (Upright)

Interpretation: ....

....

....

....

....

....

....

....

....

....

....

....

My Notes:

My Reflection:

Date: ....   Time: ....   Deck: ....

My Question: ....

....

....

....

First Card (Reversed)	Second Card (Reversed)	Third Card (Reversed)	Fourth Card (Reversed)
☐	☐	☐	☐
☐	☐	☐	☐
First Card (Upright)	Second Card (Upright)	Third Card (Upright)	Fourth Card (Upright)

Interpretation: ....

....

....

....

....

....

....

....

....

....

....

....

My Notes:

My Reflection:

Date: .... Time: .... Deck: ....

My Question:

....

....

....

First Card (Reversed) ☐	Second Card (Reversed) ☐	Third Card (Reversed) ☐	Fourth Card (Reversed) ☐
☐ First Card (Upright)	☐ Second Card (Upright)	☐ Third Card (Upright)	☐ Fourth Card (Upright)

Interpretation:

....

....

....

....

....

....

....

....

....

....

....

....

My Notes:

My Reflection:

Date: *Time:*   *Deck:*

My Question:
....
....
....
....

First Card (Reversed) ☐	Second Card (Reversed) ☐	Third Card (Reversed) ☐	Fourth Card (Reversed) ☐
☐ First Card (Upright)	☐ Second Card (Upright)	☐ Third Card (Upright)	☐ Fourth Card (Upright)

Interpretation:
....
....
....
....
....
....
....
....
....
....
....
....

My Notes:

My Reflection:

Date: Time: Deck:

My Question:

....

....

....

First Card (Reversed)	Second Card (Reversed)	Third Card (Reversed)	Fourth Card (Reversed)
☐	☐	☐	☐
☐	☐	☐	☐
First Card (Upright)	Second Card (Upright)	Third Card (Upright)	Fourth Card (Upright)

Interpretation:

....

....

....

....

....

....

....

....

....

....

My Notes:

My Reflection:

Date: _____   Time: _____   Deck: _____

My Question: _____

....

....

....

First Card (Reversed)	Second Card (Reversed)	Third Card (Reversed)	Fourth Card (Reversed)
☐	☐	☐	☐
☐	☐	☐	☐
First Card (Upright)	Second Card (Upright)	Third Card (Upright)	Fourth Card (Upright)

Interpretation: ....

....

....

....

....

....

....

....

....

....

....

....

....

My Notes:

My Reflection:

Date: _____ *Time:* _____ *Deck:* _____

My Question: _____

....

....

....

First Card (Reversed)	Second Card (Reversed)	Third Card (Reversed)	Fourth Card (Reversed)
☐	☐	☐	☐
☐	☐	☐	☐
First Card (Upright)	**Second Card** (Upright)	**Third Card** (Upright)	**Fourth Card** (Upright)

Interpretation: ....

....

....

....

....

....

....

....

....

....

....

My Notes:

My Reflection:

Date: .... *Time:* .... *Deck:* ....

My Question:

....

....

....

First Card (Reversed) ☐	Second Card (Reversed) ☐	Third Card (Reversed) ☐	Fourth Card (Reversed) ☐
☐ First Card (Upright)	☐ Second Card (Upright)	☐ Third Card (Upright)	☐ Fourth Card (Upright)

Interpretation: ....

....

....

....

....

....

....

....

....

....

....

My Notes:

_____
_____
_____
_____
_____
_____
_____
_____
_____

My Reflection:

_____
_____
_____
_____
_____
_____
_____
_____
_____
_____
_____

Date: .... *Time:* .... *Deck:* ....

My Question: ....

....

....

....

First Card (Reversed)	Second Card (Reversed)	Third Card (Reversed)	Fourth Card (Reversed)
☐	☐	☐	☐
☐	☐	☐	☐
First Card (Upright)	Second Card (Upright)	Third Card (Upright)	Fourth Card (Upright)

Interpretation: ....

....

....

....

....

....

....

....

....

....

....

....

....

My Notes:

My Reflection:

Date: .... *Time:* .... *Deck:* ....

My Question: ....

....

....

....

First Card (Reversed) ☐	Second Card (Reversed) ☐	Third Card (Reversed) ☐	Fourth Card (Reversed) ☐
☐ First Card (Upright)	☐ Second Card (Upright)	☐ Third Card (Upright)	☐ Fourth Card (Upright)

Interpretation: ....

....

....

....

....

....

....

....

....

....

....

....

My Notes:

My Reflection:

Date: _____ Time: _____ Deck: _____

My Question: _____

....

....

....

First Card (Reversed)	Second Card (Reversed)	Third Card (Reversed)	Fourth Card (Reversed)
☐	☐	☐	☐
☐	☐	☐	☐
First Card (Upright)	Second Card (Upright)	Third Card (Upright)	Fourth Card (Upright)

Interpretation: ....

....

....

....

....

....

....

....

....

....

....

....

....

My Notes:

My Reflection:

Date: _____ Time: _____ Deck: _____

My Question:

....

....

....

First Card (Reversed) ☐	Second Card (Reversed) ☐	Third Card (Reversed) ☐	Fourth Card (Reversed) ☐
☐ First Card (Upright)	☐ Second Card (Upright)	☐ Third Card (Upright)	☐ Fourth Card (Upright)

Interpretation:

....

....

....

....

....

....

....

....

....

....

....

....

....

My Notes:

My Reflection:

Date:　　　　　*Time:*　　　　　*Deck:*

My Question:

....

....

....

| First Card (Reversed) ☐ | Second Card (Reversed) ☐ | Third Card (Reversed) ☐ | Fourth Card (Reversed) ☐ |
| ☐ First Card (Upright) | ☐ Second Card (Upright) | ☐ Third Card (Upright) | ☐ Fourth Card (Upright) |

Interpretation:

....

....

....

....

....

....

....

....

....

....

....

My Notes:

My Reflection:

Date: .... *Time:* .... *Deck:* ....

My Question:

....

....

....

First Card (Reversed)	Second Card (Reversed)	Third Card (Reversed)	Fourth Card (Reversed)
☐	☐	☐	☐
☐	☐	☐	☐
First Card (Upright)	Second Card (Upright)	Third Card (Upright)	Fourth Card (Upright)

Interpretation:

....

....

....

....

....

....

....

....

....

....

....

....

....

My Notes:

My Reflection:

Date: _____ *Time:* _____ *Deck:* _____

My Question:

....

....

....

First Card (Reversed) ☐	Second Card (Reversed) ☐	Third Card (Reversed) ☐	Fourth Card (Reversed) ☐
☐ First Card (Upright)	☐ Second Card (Upright)	☐ Third Card (Upright)	☐ Fourth Card (Upright)

Interpretation:

....

....

....

....

....

....

....

....

....

....

....

My Notes:

My Reflection:

Date: _____ *Time:* _____ *Deck:* _____

My Question: _____

....

....

....

First Card (Reversed)	Second Card (Reversed)	Third Card (Reversed)	Fourth Card (Reversed)
☐	☐	☐	☐
☐	☐	☐	☐
First Card (Upright)	**Second Card** (Upright)	**Third Card** (Upright)	**Fourth Card** (Upright)

Interpretation: ....

....

....

....

....

....

....

....

....

....

....

....

....

My Notes:

My Reflection:

Date: Time: Deck:

My Question:

....

....

....

First Card (Reversed) ☐	Second Card (Reversed) ☐	Third Card (Reversed) ☐	Fourth Card (Reversed) ☐
☐ First Card (Upright)	☐ Second Card (Upright)	☐ Third Card (Upright)	☐ Fourth Card (Upright)

Interpretation:

....

....

....

....

....

....

....

....

....

....

....

My Notes:

My Reflection:

Date: Time: Deck:

My Question:

....

....

....

First Card (Reversed)	Second Card (Reversed)	Third Card (Reversed)	Fourth Card (Reversed)
☐	☐	☐	☐
☐	☐	☐	☐
First Card (Upright)	Second Card (Upright)	Third Card (Upright)	Fourth Card (Upright)

Interpretation:

....

....

....

....

....

....

....

....

....

....

....

....

My Notes:

My Reflection:

Date: .... _Time:_ .... _Deck:_ ....

My Question:

....

....

....

First Card (Reversed)	Second Card (Reversed)	Third Card (Reversed)	Fourth Card (Reversed)
☐	☐	☐	☐
☐	☐	☐	☐
First Card (Upright)	Second Card (Upright)	Third Card (Upright)	Fourth Card (Upright)

Interpretation: ....

....

....

....

....

....

....

....

....

....

....

....

My Notes:

My Reflection:

Date: *Time:*   *Deck:*

My Question:

....

....

....

First Card (Reversed)	Second Card (Reversed)	Third Card (Reversed)	Fourth Card (Reversed)
☐	☐	☐	☐
☐	☐	☐	☐
First Card (Upright)	**Second Card** (Upright)	**Third Card** (Upright)	**Fourth Card** (Upright)

Interpretation: ....

....

....

....

....

....

....

....

....

....

....

....

My Notes:

My Reflection:

Impressum / Imprint:
Florian Reichl | Urbanstr 65 | 10967 Berlin | Germany
info@frdesign.org

Made in the USA
Las Vegas, NV
19 November 2023

81123656R10121